DEEPER THAN FLESH

DEEPER THAN FLESH

A JOURNEY THROUGH SELF-LOVE & DISCOVERY

BRIANNA FRIERSON

Deeper Than Flesh: A Journey Through Self-love & Discovery

Copyright © 2020 Brianna Frierson

All rights reserved. No part of this book may be reproduced or transmitted in any form or by any means, electronic or mechanical, including photocopying, recording, or by any information stored in a retrieval system without written permission from the author, except for the inclusion of brief quotes in a review.

Scriptures are taken from the Holy Bible, King James Version ©, KJV ©. Copyright © 1973, 1978, 1984, 2011 by Biblica, Inc.™ Used by permission. All rights reserved worldwide.

Edited By: Forlanda Anderson

Paperback ISBN: 9780578808451

Printed in the United States of America

Contents

Acknowledgements		v
Introduction		1
1.	The Road Less Traveled	2
2.	Face It	10
3.	Re-evaluate EVERYTHING!	17
4.	Soul Ties Never Lie	22
5.	A New Found Love	28
6.	Clear View	32
7.	Trust Your Instincts	35
8.	Chase Yourself	38
9.	Old Habits Will Not Open New Doors	43
10.	Reciprocity	47
11.	Giving Birth to the Woman I Want to be	52
12.	Masterpiece I AM.	55
13.	Rebirth	57

Acknowledgements

For the hearts that broke and the crowns that never dropped. To my mother, Tracey, and father, Michael, I love you with all my heart. Thank you for loving and guiding me through it all.

To Jevette, thank you for filling me up with love during my darkest hour. You helped me to see that there is joy in temporary pain.

To my family, I love each one of you and pray that you fulfill your wildest dreams. To my Lord and Savior, thank you for always pouring out blessings far greater than I can receive, and teaching me to love every part of life's processes.

Introduction

Celibacy is a valid choice. It is not primarily about isolating oneself from temptation, because temptation is a part of life. It's about being able to make a conscious decision on whether or not sexual encounters you engage in are benefiting your soul.

If I knew then that I would choose the option of being celibate, I'd probably laugh and say, "Yeah right. Me?" Revisiting my past I learned that the way we view ourselves is heavily reflected on the people we associate with, who we date, and what we allow in our space. Celibacy has allowed me to tap into every sense and gain a new perspective on life. The beauty in practicing celibacy is taking back the power that was stolen and healing old wounds that felt like permanent scars. In life, we experience love, joy, happiness, and fulfillment when we are surrounded by genuine people and situations.

I

THE ROAD LESS TRAVELED

> "Blessed is she who believed that the Lord would fulfill His promises to her." – Psalms 1:45

I have been single and celibate for over two years. I always say that I'm celibate, not dead. This simply means that I am human and experience temptation, but having self-control and a deeper purpose outweighs any sexual urge. Embarking on this journey, I quickly realized that the word of God, along with living out celibacy, can be powerful for others. I received many reactions when discussing my journey, some more memorable than others. My parents were proud and said this would be a good example for people my age, but still said, "This is not a form of birth control, so be careful, not carefree." Out of respect for my mother and father, I took the advice with a grain of salt but knew the only parent that could truly guide me through was God.

At that moment, I realized I would be on this journey alone. However, God would never let you leave point A without having point B waiting on you. I knew that if I were to be committed to this part of my life, I would have to be ALL in. Any decision you make in life will solely be yours. You cannot live counting on the opinions or blueprints others have set out for themselves. If I worried about people, things, and situations, I would "lose" while transforming and would not heed to what God was trying to tell me all along. Celibacy for me meant far more than just wiping out sex, but toxicity as a whole.

The biggest reality check came from the guys that I showed interest in and revealing to them my seriousness toward being successful in my new walk. It was not easy for them to grasp the concept of a female not willing to sacrifice herself to make them happy sexually. The disappointing reality was the mindset boys had. They viewed my standards as if it were the ultimate challenge and tried to break my status and lead me into temptation. I knew for certain that no one on Earth could allow me to give myself to them without my permission.

The constant reminder that a millennial embarking on an unconventional way of life would be a surprise to most, was a reward within itself. It allowed me to reflect on how narrow-minded I was, as well as the hype behind our over-sexualized culture. It is very important to know the difference between having sex to pass time and making love knowing the person you are submitting yourself to. This, without a doubt, can create a soul tie far beyond human understanding.

I was tired of giving myself to people that were temporary fillers. Not just in the context of sex, but also my time. We never know how valuable our time is until something comes to an end — a relationship, friendship, or even a life. Our human mind cannot fathom the thought of time wasted because we often think that we make the right decisions as individuals. The truth behind our decisions causes us to act in ways we normally would not toward those we love. The perfect example is during my first serious relationship. I was young and in love, but my mother and father could see right through my ex's ways. My mother was very vocal in letting me know that this too shall pass. They knew that his type would not appreciate a good thing, even if it was right in front of him. I remember my ex was very drawn to what my mother's thoughts were of him. One particular talk between them stuck with him throughout the course of our relationship. She simply told him, "game peeps game and honey, I've played the game before." He told me the conversation went well even after she said this. He questioned the meaning behind her statement, in which she replied, "in due time."

You see, the ones who truly love and care about us can see the intentions of people that come into our lives with ulterior motives. We are blind to what we think is best for us, which in most cases can lead to disaster. It is OK to love someone, but after so long we have to learn to heed to what signs are being shown. When a man is dating you, don't be so willing to jump right into sex, give yourself time to discover one another. Sex without a doubt complicates the most genuine bond; you cannot be properly courted if you've given the other person nothing to look forward to. As a millennial, I've witnessed fast-paced relationships and young couples engaging in ways of that of a husband and wife dynamic. I've witnessed young women bend over backward to please their boyfriend and even going as far as putting off the things they adored before the relationship became heavy. Growing up, I was always told three key rules:

1. Never half step the things you care about.
2. Always keep God first in all that you do.
3. Never play the fool for someone, not even the ones you love.

Never lose sight of your why.

I can't even count how often I see people forget their dreams and who they are when they enter a new relationship. It's so easy to lose sight of yourself when distractions come easily in the form of the void you've been desiring. One thing is certain: the choices we make in life are just that — a choice. I can attest to losing focus during my first serious relationship. Everything was about "us," and forgetting we were individuals first was the biggest mistake. I would be lying if I didn't say that it is easy to lose focus when you are "in love" and even lust.

When God formed us, he knew our purpose and what steps we should take to achieve it. Figuring out your purpose does not come easy and cannot be bought. It takes hard work, dedication, prayer, and love for what you do. Your "why" is in the very fiber of your being. Never sleep on yourself or create a pattern of distractions while still figuring out your why. It is more rewarding to know yourself and to work toward your goals than to lose sight of yourself and to gain a heart of regret later on in life. I am by no means saying you can't be happy in a relationship and successful at the same time; however, it is possible. I hear so many couples say that if their partner had found them years ago the interest would have ceased. People always think it's so painful to lose the one you value. In reality, the most painful thing is losing yourself in the process of valuing someone too much and forgetting that YOU are special too. You are a priority and are worthy of everything you desire. Always put yourself first and remember that your inner happiness sets the tone for every encounter you experience in life, including the relationships you foster, the career path you choose, and the way you perceive people's opinions of you. Self-love is a remedy to blocking all things toxic that try to negate your journey. As you continue to honor, respect, and nurture yourself, you'll see how easy it is to discern what is for you and what is not. You should be unwavering in your commitment to loving yourself each day. You are special because you alone were put on this Earth to walk a distinct journey that God sees fit for you. No matter what obstacles you face or opinions people have, remember only you can validate yourself. Each trial you face shapes you into the best version of yourself. Be proud and walk boldly as the masterpiece you are.

Always keep God first in all that you do.

As a millennial, some of us tend to forget the meaning of the term "humble." When things are on the "up and up" we lose sight of who gave us the victory after the storm, and when times are rough we act out. Every inch of life requires guidance. Why not receive the best God has to offer? I'll admit my faults of thinking simple things in life, like going to work and completing a shift, would be easy. How foolish was I to forget or think so small, the moments that I didn't think I needed God and guidance usually became my most dramatic experiences. I vividly remember growing up in the church and taking pride in having a relationship with God during the early years of my adolescence. It was not until I was a teenager that I realized just how important it was to speak with God, even about the little things. God already knows every detail of your life. I even became partially a cliché of the, "I'm in a relationship now, I'll miss church today," club. I should've known then by witnessing my character become flawed, that I was becoming something I wasn't. However, my support system played a major role during this time of my life. I've learned that life is so much sweeter when you have a friend and support system that will never leave you and will help guide you back to reality. God has blessed so many aspects of my life and I feel more alive today than I've ever felt before. Remember, broken pieces can become blessed masterpieces if you let God be in control of each brushstroke.

> Never play the fool for someone, not even those you love.

I never knew the true meaning of "wolves in sheep's clothing" until my first heartbreak and after parting ways with fake friendships. Between the experience of both, I never viewed them as a "loss," but as a lesson. Life is simply lessons, both intricate and plain tests that can ultimately build or destroy our character. We all know the cost of staying in something that has an expiration date, yet we all entertain the thought of it. It is quite normal to want to protect, help, or love someone, even if our intuition tells us to cut ties. There is a thin line between loving someone and causing harm to your spirit in the process. As humans we are very acquainted with our energy, if you sense something is not sitting well with your spirit, don't force it. It is a sign that you should not follow through with the issue at hand. Trust your instincts and give yourself space. You don't owe anyone anything; however, you owe it to yourself to be real about your role in the matter. Never allow anyone to take advantage of your kindness, as it is meant to diminish your being in subtle ways that are hard to detect. We forget that some bonds are like subscriptions and only YOU are in control of canceling it.

2

FACE IT

> "I consider that our present sufferings are not worth comparing with the glory that will be revealed to us." – Romans 8:18

There comes a time in our lives when we have to take ownership of our actions and realize that we are part to blame in our demise. Making the wrong choices in men and longing for a deeper connection ultimately led me to what is without a doubt the best decision I ever could have made. I've never considered myself a hopeless romantic, but a young woman that sees the good in most. Having my heart broken a few times and coming to my senses, I knew I couldn't go backward. When you've reached your "rock bottom," no matter the situation, I firmly believe that

God is shaking your foundation for a new beginning.

I let go of my fears and doubts and faced them. I started my journey in celibacy three years ago and life has changed tremendously. My circle became smaller and my tolerance for nonsense decreased. Celibacy is not just a choice that affects your sexual experiences, it projects onto your entire being. I can't stress enough to the people I've had a dialogue with about the topic of taking care of yourself first. Work on any parts of your life that you feel is lacking or needs improvement, instead of looking for acceptance or blockage from reality by falling into the arms of a stranger.

Starting with self-evaluation is the foundation for taking ownership of your mistakes. One cannot blame everyone else for life catching them off guard. It is the same as going to church and you are writing the sermon down, but you never think to open the Bible for the answers. There is no excuse to ignore the tools lying right in front of us — even if we resort to using our cell phones to read the Bible, as so many millennials do. There is absolutely nothing wrong with this, as long as you are learning.

Facing self-doubt, pain, generational curses, and adversity start with what's projecting from the inside out. The first step is recognizing that there is room for growth, which we all could gain from. As long as you are working toward obtaining the best version of yourself, everything else, good or bad, will fall off or follow. Our biggest flaw is concerning ourselves with the thoughts or opinions of others as if they are attached to us. Once you realize you have to shed certain people like dry skin, life becomes a smoother ride.

Throughout my own celibacy journey, I have been asked numerous times about what I hope to gain from it. Initially, I would say I am taking it day by day and would sit in awe of the fact that I hadn't even thought that far. Speaking my truth, I had to realize that being newly celibate did not come with a manual that reads, "do this and make sure to stop this habit." Becoming celibate for me came as a no brainer, but it was not a subtle change. I went full-on cold turkey and questioned my "why." Facing my friends and family as they asked me if I was OK and told me that they didn't see how I could get through this was both comical and a reality check. It showed me that the mind is so powerful and that once you set your mind to something, the opinions fostered by anyone other than you does not matter. Out of all of the things I was asked and told, one encounter that stood out was from a coworker of mine. I remember we would have so many interesting conversations, but this time she bluntly asked, "Why are you doing this when you are so young and have so much love to give out?" I knew what this person meant, but I decided to ask to avoid assuming.

Her exact words were, "I couldn't do it. I've never done that because I love the thrill of it and in my prime, there is no way I would cut sex completely out, especially not in college." At this very moment, I realized that the art of celibacy was seen as a death sentence for a huge percentage of people, even those much older than me. It is not by chance that we encounter people who have different views than our own. This notion doesn't make them weak and it doesn't place you on a pedestal, it simply gives light to just how our experiences shape our future.

Facing it means so many things. At that moment I faced a person whom I respected, disagreed with my decision to become celibate, and praised their temptation. My celibacy journey has increased my level of strength while encountering temptations in the simplest forms, like being in the same room as someone you are attracted to. We don't realize that even being around those we love while they introduce us to new people can be an ordeal within itself. The perfect example of this is while I was in my last year of college and my friends and I would meet up. I love my friends dearly and wouldn't dream of shaming them for their individual choices in life, even in my new walk. There were so many times I would sit and watch them roll blunts in rotation, talk about who they had sex with, and of course how they commend me for being celibate, but turn around and question the purpose behind my celibacy journey. I'd always have to go deeper into my why, but even this allowed the opportunity for growth and to affirm my journey. Many people have sex to fill a void or succumb to temporary urges. This solves nothing — no gain, no real love connection, and no self-validation. You cannot sex your way through pain that started with false promises through the same strokes, even if it is from another person.

When you face your deepest insecurities, pain, and fear through self-evaluation, it allows your purpose to give light to your experience and helps express your truth.

Reflection Questions:

What are you facing in this season?

_____

_____

How are you going to improve it?

_____

_____

What are your goals for the outcome?

_____

_____

Now, think about a time that you were presented with temptation. How did you handle it?

_____

_____

Are you happy with your decision?

_____

_____

3

RE-EVALUATE EVERYTHING!

> "Do not conform to the pattern of this world, but be transformed by the renewing of your mind." – Romans 12:2

Some of the first steps I took were re-evaluating my priorities and putting my own needs and wants at the forefront. As a woman, I feel that for most of us it is second nature to put others before ourselves. It's not a flaw or a weakness, it's life. However, when your habit of pleasing others is draining your very being, it is time to re-evaluate. Conforming to a pattern that is not healthy for your personal growth is not only hurtful but can be dangerous in many aspects of life. One thing to keep in mind is that pouring so much life into others will leave our cups either half full or empty. We all want our cups to runneth over, so don't forget that you are in charge of how much is left in your cup.

Re-evaluating everything was not easy. I had to let go of friendships that were hanging on by a thread and take a serious mental note of what relationships were healthy for the woman I want to become. It is so easy to say we are going to do something, but I don't believe there is one person on this earth that is prepared to detoxify those they may love out of their routine. I wrote down all of the things I felt were important to have in a healthy bond, in both relationships and friendships.

The biggest reality check was the guys I noticed I was attracting or entertaining. I always prided myself on saying, "I don't have a type," when in reality I was falling for the same emptiness. My reasoning for saying emptiness instead of humans is simple: a person cannot give you pure love or fill you up if they are empty. Realizing my contributions to this demise showed me that I had a void within me as well. As tough as it may be to hear the truth, it is important to own your reality. The guys I was into were attractive but lacked the very thing I knew God had for me — passion. You see, to truly love someone you have to have a passion for them. You cannot half-step in your efforts because even the purest love requires work.

I had been in a relationship for so long that I forgot what it meant to truly enjoy my own company.

Sadly, this is a truth for many of us. We cling on to friends and relationships that have passed their expiration date. When you are newly single or no longer hanging out with the same people, it forces you to take time for yourself, which can feel like a foreign place. Don't approach this as a bad place to be. You should never be ashamed to enjoy your own company. I can say that based on my experience, it feels so liberating. I'd notice how people would stare at me trying to figure out if I was alone or meeting someone. Before coming to grips with my new way of life, I knew I had to re-evaluate my thoughts. I re-evaluated any negative thoughts that crossed my mind with a positive affirmation and left room for positive influences.

I'm here to tell you that if you ever feel alone in the company of yourself, remember that God is always with you and you are a reflection of Him, so you are never alone. When you re-evaluate your priorities, always remember that you are always at the top of the list. If it means closing chapters that are overdue, so be it! It would suffice to be in a clear space alone than to be in a crowded room full of fog and uncertainty. There is nothing more worthwhile in this life than to not only exist but to live wholeheartedly.

Taking your life back is not an option, so why would you settle for anything less than you deserve? Tolerating people in your life to avoid being the only one in the room is not an excuse. When you feel yourself in this predicament, turn to God and pray in fullness about your thoughts and feelings because it'll never fall on deaf ears. Reclaiming your authority in your life and not conforming to be someone's doormat or second choice propels greatness in every aspect. You are worth so much more than that. When you own your worth no one could ever put a price tag on it.

Reflection Questions:

Do you spend time alone?

_____

_____

Do you view being alone as negative or positive? Why?

_____

_____

What is one thing in your life that has become a priority that you may need to re-evaluate?

4

SOUL TIES NEVER LIE

> "I focus on this one thing: Forgetting the past and looking forward to what lies ahead." – Philippians 3:13

Initially, when I chose to become celibate I made a list of the pros and cons of what the journey could offer. One thing I knew would be a great relief is the conscious mind I gained from knowing I wouldn't fall into temptation for future soul ties. What is a soul tie? A soul tie is an emotional bond or connection that unites you with someone else. You can become bound to a person through your soul. In this world, we fall into the trap of giving people ourselves without knowing them. You see, to know a person and to truly know who they are, are two completely different things. You can tell yourself each day that this person wants you for your mind or internal assets, but when denial slips away, don't forget that God always gives us signs early on. The more people you intertwine with sexually, the more spirits latch onto you. Picture yourself getting to know someone and getting to a point of comfort and introducing sex into your new bond, then he or she starts to unmask their true nature. This alone is a wakeup call and testament to trust your instincts.

The problem with a lot of people in the world, not just singling out millennials, is the lack of care we have about those we have sex with. Often it comes so easy to let the physical nature of sex overshadow the spiritual aspect. It is not healthy to be consumed with the idea that your body count does not define your being. In reality, your soul takes on the characteristics of the people you sleep with. As easy as it sounds to rid yourself of a person after the deed is done, you could never fully rid your soul of them like a bad habit.

We should treat our souls with more care, it is the closest direct line we have with God next to our hearts. In a world full of materialistic and superficial things, we hold our belongings over nurturing what's on the inside of us. As sad as it sounds, we have to reassess our priorities before we run to a place of no return. Taking care of yourself from the inside reflects what is seen on the outside. We always hear the term, "you are what you eat," but never say, "you are who you sleep with." The people you choose to have sex with are ultimately a reflection of who you are. We shy away from the thought of being changed by those we allow into our space. I am here to say that it is OK to realize someone has projected themselves into your space, as long as you save yourself before the explosion happens. Even those we love can create a negative soul tie for us, but ultimately it is in our hands to start the process of cutting it.

The emphasis on committing to a journey is to enjoy your life fully as a single person, which requires you to know who you are before you bond with someone else. A lot of us are aiming at the wrong targets and tend to get excited about physical things. Imagine jumping into bed with someone only because he or she is attractive to you, but you haven't grown to know him or her. Quit making your body an easy target. No man or woman truly wants someone who has been used up. Allowing people into our lives and leading into the process of dating should be like a job interview. You know, the kind leading into a salary job. During the first round, it should simply be a determinant of whether or not you're on the same level. This will help you avoid bringing unnecessary people around those you love and creating simple soul ties. We often give unqualified people second interviews because we think there is a shortage in our company. There is nothing wrong with dating, but ask yourself, is the person I'm dating bringing glory to God? Never start a bond on a fragile foundation.

The essence of a fragile foundation can stem from merely making the other person's outer appearance the main trait that makes the difference on whether or not you give them a chance or one thing that escaped their mouth that turned you off. We all have been shallow to a certain extent in regards to vetting someone during the dating process, only to find that we may have chosen the wrong candidate. However, if we use the right discernment in the beginning and not take a back seat to what our flesh desires, we will be less susceptible to a destructive outcome. We also need to realize each human being is a spiritual being. Just because a person's outer appearance is well put together does not mean they are on the inside. In situations where you are ready to date or go to the next level with a special someone, don't rush the process. There is a reason for allowing things to flow naturally and not forcing a bond to happen. It is both fate and God's protection.

Reflection Questions:

    Have you ever experienced a soul tie?

Do you think of this person often or have sporadic dreams of them?

What are you going to do to come out of it?

Did you create a barrier to break it?

5

A NEW FOUND LOVE

"Love always protects, always trusts, always perseveres, LOVE never fails." – 1 Corinthians 13:7-8

The beauty within my journey is rediscovering myself and gaining a deeper love for Christ. As cliché as it may sound, you don't realize what you have until it's gone. I wasn't aware of the void I felt in my heart until I allowed that space to be filled by someone with substance, genuine love, and care. Who better to trust with your heart than God? No one. We often search for love in all the wrong places in hopes that we will somehow trip and fall into the arms of our soulmate, and we forget that God made it so easy to love Him. This is not to say that effort for showing your love for God should be minimal.

What I am saying is that you should be more open to God's never-ending love than searching for love in man.

Redirecting my focus on the man upstairs helped me humble myself and aim toward building bonds with genuine people. It is so important to notice that when you aim toward pleasing God, without hesitation, He alters your life beyond measure. Circumstances that I may have seen as issues or traits about myself that I began to over-analyze, developed into hindsight fruition. I always try to see the good in people, even if they have wronged me in some way. However, after experiencing confirmation that my concerns were valid, I knew certain things I would not tolerate. No matter how far we try to run in the opposite direction from God and our morals, life will get you together faster than a blink of an eye.

The best moments of peace we experience are in quietness with God. I was so busy with work, social life, and family matters that I neglected the times of stillness that I needed. My head was filled with things I had to get done, where I had to go, and even small things that should not have been on my mind. I realized soon enough that this moment was God's way of saying, "be calm, be still, and focus on me." As humans, we concern ourselves with keeping up appearances and often pleasing others so much that we don't take time for ourselves. Our thoughts can either own us or guide us; by this, I simply mean we are in control of what we allow to fill our minds. We are visionary creatures and even the slightest image can affect a memory that we've suppressed. Never fight against relaxing or being still because it is a form of releasing bad energy.

Always know that God will never have you repeat a test you have not passed. In a season of uncertainty, where you may question God's timing and why things are being removed, just know that season has ended for your betterment. You are worthy of all things good. He wants to ensure you are ready before you receive the very things you've prayed for. Think about it, what if you received the relationship, dream job, or house you've always wanted before you were ready. You'd be destructive to it. Pull back and stop being so obsessed with the idea of having something you already know He has promised you. Be confident in who you are in the present because you are a gift and the energy you exude will attract those greater outcomes. I want you to have a house that's a home, a relationship that fulfills you because both of you are whole as individuals, and a career that elevates your lifestyle and doesn't stress you out. This very reasoning is why the wait is so important.

Reflection Questions:

What are some things you need to release?

_____

_____

How do you show it with actions?

_____

_____

What is love to you?

_____

_____

6

CLEAR VIEW

> "The eye is the lamp of the body. So, if your eye is healthy, your whole body will be full of light." – Matthew 6:22

Throughout life, we tend to only focus our attention on the things we want to see and remain in denial about the things that are right in front of us. The worst decision we could ever make is choosing to ignore signs that God gives us as warnings to avoid total disaster. I can testify to noticing this within short-lived friendships and failed relationships. I chose to keep my blinders on hoping for a better outcome from those I loved and the bonds we shared. Even throughout the process of writing this book, I had to reflect on a few issues from my past that led to disasters. The great thing about growth is just how much it forces us to mature and flourish as individuals. As I consider some of the guys I dated, it is apparent that red flags were in front of me from the very beginning. For instance, I always knew that my faith in God would not cease, so being in a relationship with someone who spoke negatively about Him would not suffice. In high school I dated a guy that finally admitted he was an atheist — he was my friend so I asked him how this came to be. His answer didn't settle well with my spirit. It's not that he wasn't good enough or that I looked down on his walk, but I received an overwhelming feeling when his true nature came out. The red flags were so visible like that of the brightest red lipstick a woman can own.

I admit that I was intimate with this person, which in time clouded my discernment throughout us dating. This very case is one of many examples that led me to celibacy. You see, we worry so much as millennials about the physical, that we drift away from how people treat us and our growth. There is not one person on Earth worth stunting your growth for. If you ever cross paths with that person, you might as well turn your back and walk the other way for your own happiness. We are infatuated with the idea of sexual healing while not even knowing if this person cares for your heart or your thoughts. We are more than the sum of our sexual encounters, the number of partners we please, and the multiple convenient options within our phones.

As I journey through what true discernment means, I find myself knowing what a guy wants before he even speaks. It is not a prejudgment or assumption, but if you look with a clear view, you'll notice that a person can speak volumes without opening their mouth. Discernment requires a clear thought process and open heart to accept what life throws at you, whether good or bad. It is like having the ultimate shield in a battle that lies ahead — you know what's coming, but remain confident in your approach. Discernment also comes with humility. It is vital to not boast about this aspect of your celibacy because we are all equal in God's eyes. Being celibate is like having a golden ticket and inside, an understanding with God that no one else can grasp unless they decided to walk the same path.

7

TRUST YOUR INSTINCTS

"Faith can move mountains." – Matthew 17:20

Trusting your instincts is a must, but we so easily shy away from the gift of it. Our instincts are what separate us from danger, unwarranted responses, and some of life's biggest curveballs. Although we know it's resourceful and for our betterment to trust our initial feeling, we do the opposite. In regards to matters of the heart, we may get an inkling that a red flag is waving right in front of us, but we ignore it with thoughts of "potential." Seeing potential in someone does not mean you turn off your natural senses to them to avoid the obvious outcome. One of the best examples is when your person of interest is inconsistent. If a person says they will make time for you and turn around only to say, "I didn't guarantee that," save yourself the trouble and make them the option they've made you. A person is only as good as their word. Ask yourself if you'd be comfortable allowing someone close to your heart who can't keep their word.

Your very being is valuable. Don't settle for less just to feel wanted. Remember you are always loved and worth it. I say this because we easily forget that Christ chose you specifically when he made the ultimate sacrifice. If a man or a woman isn't treating you with respect or care, leave the situation immediately because you owe them nothing. Don't allow a red flag to become a pattern that could only grow into a bigger problem. The same value and effort you've put into gaining the attention of that person belong to you. Why would you take away from being the best version of yourself to give to an unappreciative person? We forget that blessings also come in moments when things are taken away from us. For instance, God will block someone out of your life that you may find attractive to protect you from their very nature. Have you ever caught yourself years later looking at a person you grew to like and said, "thank you, God!" We all have. Even while trying to offset feelings you grew, you'll realize that in those bitter moments, God was bringing you full circle for your very purpose.

There are things you have to reflect on as an individual before you start running into horizontal relationships. You have to work on your relationship with God and have a better prayer life. You are never too cool to pray. Prayer still changes things, both big and small, God will see it through. As humans, we forget that completion is necessary before you can give energy to someone else. How can you pour into someone else and forget yourself? When you love yourself your energy becomes contagious. Invest in yourself, take care of yourself, and know that you are valuable to God.

Prayer is in direct alignment with discernment. Ask God if this person is right for you. He will show you, without a doubt. Don't allow your flesh to take the front seat on what your spirit has shouted all along. You may see a beautiful girl or a handsome man and say, "they have it all together." That feeds your perception of them, which is deception. When you let your spirit lead, superficial things can never blind you. Consider asking important questions. For example, what are their intentions? Are they family-oriented? Do they have a relationship with God? Are they a user? Get to know the real person and it will save you a lot of heartaches.

8

CHASE YOURSELF

"Guard your heart above all else, for it determines the course of your life." – Proverbs 4:23

Throughout my journey with celibacy, I learned to revisit things that fed my soul — one being this very book and being creative. I was able and willing to free myself of putting time into others that my spirit craved. Whether you were in a relationship and dialed back on doing things for yourself or you've allowed adversities to take over your happiness, once you pour love and light into yourself, things can only manifest positively around you. You'll be so busy loving yourself and finding new things that please you, that when an opportunity that you have longed for comes, it'll be effortless. Stop throwing a pity party for yourself over the things that you don't have just yet because they will happen. Spend time getting to know yourself.

Take advantage of "me time." You deserve it. There is nothing in this world better than being able to treat yourself. Take yourself out for dinner or pamper yourself. You train people on how to treat you by how you treat yourself. Going out in public alone should never be awkward for you. If you don't enjoy owning a room alone, how could you conquer one confidently with someone else? We tend to crave acceptance and feel small when entering new spaces. Here's a tip: DON'T. Those who are meant to will connect with you solely based on who you are. Be good to yourself, and through your journey, you'll recognize the things that serve you and things that mean you harm. I can admit that while dating myself, it was easy to see qualities that make me unique and ones that I should sharpen. Being single and celibate was and still is the best reward I could have given myself. Like any other process, your approach can make or break the outcome. Cater to yourself, honey! Your confidence cannot be bought — it is earned for you by you! Own it.

One key factor in loving yourself is owning your flaws and either working on it or wearing it with confidence. For instance, if you tend to make false promises, that's a habit you must work on because it will spiral out of control. If it's a physical trait that you are wanting to fix, do it at your own cost. Don't change your appearance to fit in or take the easy route. God made us all perfect in his eyes and the very thing you obsess over is the very thing that makes you stand out.

Let go of being prideful and discern the difference between arrogance and confidence. There is beauty in knowing you deserve the best and going for it, but don't stick your nose up at people because they are in a different stage of life than you are. God allows us to cross paths with people who are the opposite of us to help us grow and stretch our outlook on life. Some of the deepest conversations I've had were with people I met who were completely different in their approach to life. It is in simple moments like those that we realize just how mysterious God's work can be. You can easily broaden your own views and open up to a diverse range of things just by meeting someone.

Don't waste time on what could've been because what God has for you will never miss you. Take that trip. Read that book. Go see that movie. Make that film or YouTube Channel. Stack your bank account. You'll realize that there's power in chasing yourself. When you are happy with who you are, if a breakup or switch up happens you won't allow it to break you. Be grounded in your purpose and a relationship will be an accessory, not a necessity. Give yourself the freedom to live and not stay captive to an idea that isn't realistic.

During my journey, I've learned a lot from my friends and vice versa. They would come to me for advice and just to vent when needed. Some still can't grapple with the thought of closing off the sexual side of myself for a greater purpose. I always let them know the basics of having a clear mindset when it comes to men's intentions because sex was not in the way. I truly adore my friends and love that they all come from a diverse range of backgrounds. You should surround yourself with people that pour into you while you do the same for them. If the exchange between you and those you call friends isn't beneficial, subtract yourself from the situation. No one has time to allow anyone to take up free space in their life. I also began to see myself full circle in the people I hung around. The old saying, "you are who you surround yourself with," is so valid, regardless if you are celibate or not. You can't expect positive change entertaining negative friendships. You owe it to yourself to engage in "ships" that are residual and won't sink.

Reflection Questions:

    Do you enjoy time by yourself?

_____

_____

Have you chased others more than you've chased yourself?

_____

_____

What activities would you like to experience by yourself?

_____

_____

9

OLD HABITS WILL NOT OPEN NEW DOORS

"And give no opportunity to the devil" –
Ephesians 4:27

It's easy to go back because it is familiar while going forward is a foreign land to us. Many of us block our chances of meeting our soulmate because we are stuck on stupid. When you realize the calling God has on your life you can't allow yourself to be held back in a mediocre relationship. The devil knows your mind and how easy it can be for confusing thoughts to race in your head. Don't give him the satisfaction, be strong, and speak positive affirmations. If you stopped communicating with someone because they have wronged you, let them go — completely. If you receive a text or a phone call don't answer. It's not being mean or childish, it is putting an end to a curse that could stretch far past your lifetime. Don't allow your flesh to take the driver's side in your journey through life because you'll crash each time.

Stop voluntarily blocking your blessings for temporary people. People aren't always connected to your destiny. Romanticizing about future relationships is tricky; however, it is your approach that can lead to negative outcomes. There is no problem with having an idea of what you want because you have every right to do so. Don't rush because you see people in your social circles, social media, or even in your family succeed in a relationship. You never know their struggles, so don't be quick to judge and compare your happiness to what others have. Your joy is not measured by or for others — it is YOURS ONLY.

If you feel yourself criticizing your own life and where you are, simply stop, breathe, and remember that this very moment was meant for your greater good. You are anointed in greatness. You are loved, and when walking in your purpose, things find you, not the other way around. The law of attraction is real: you attract what you are. You may have met people that made you question their intentions. That could be a sign that you are simply not ready or happy with yourself. Work on your insecurities and the traits within yourself that deter your self-confidence and you'll attract people of higher vibrations. Get yourself in sync with what you aspire to be and trust that it will be reciprocated in due time.

Lastly, remember that giving up so easily is a lazy trait. Realistically if you can give up on your aspirations and love, you'll continue the trend. Giving up begins with a thought, which could lead to actions. Block this thought from your subconscious. You are worth the wait. Why rush a process that maximizes your outcome? Nothing worth significant value is made overnight. Giving up is what people who don't want your light to shine wish for. Don't give them the satisfaction. Ask God to guide your thoughts and footsteps, and it will be the best decision you've ever made.

Reflection Questions:

What negative thoughts are you experiencing?

How are you handling them?

_____

_____

Take time out of your day for yourself and write five positive things that happened to you today.

_____

_____

10

RECIPROCITY

> Therefore, whatever you want men to do to you, do also to them, for this is the Law and the Prophets." – Matthew 7:12

Have you ever felt like you've given your whole heart to someone only to be returned void? Well, this is not the definition of reciprocity. Rule number one: Never give your best to someone that views you as less. Love and void are on two opposite ends of the spectrum and can never cross when someone truly loves you. God did not create you to feel unloved. There should never be a lack of love, for He gives it in abundance. When you are in a relationship or dating, both parties should be sensitive to one another's feelings. Absorbing energy from someone other than yourself is a surreal feeling; without speaking, you can sense a person's emotions. Good and bad energy can bounce off of you, especially dealing with matters of the heart.

The word of God says, "Do unto others as you would have them do unto you (Matthew 7:12)." This also applies to the actions that sum up reciprocity. You cannot call any form of a relationship healthy if only one party is making the effort. There is nothing more crushing to the heart than to give your all in a relationship and receive nothing in return.

People are more than how they appear and it is important to explore the depths of someone's mind before going "all in." Don't be afraid to ask questions that reveal their emotional and intellectual intelligence. If you ask a question and receive an answer you don't agree with, that's OK. However, if it's turned around on you and the person flips and asks, "why?" in a passive-aggressive manner, that should tell you something. Understand that you will not agree with everything a person does and says, but the approach is key. I have dealt with both aggressive and passive-aggressive guys. It taught me more about how I react in certain situations and how my range of experiences weighed on me. One guy I was talking to was aggressive, meaning everything was a competition to him, even the need to be right in every conversation. It could be a conversation about our city's growth or the weather, and oh don't get me started on sports! Like many other diversified women, I enjoy sports, so naturally, I like to engage in conversations about it here and there. He had to be right when it came to his favorite sports team and who was going to the Super Bowl. It's fine to have a little friendly competition, but when you belittle a person to uplift your denial, things have gone too far.

Realistically we have high expectations in the beginning, no matter how much we own it. It's not to say that one incident like this is the reason for cutting someone off; however, it is a blueprint for what may lie ahead. Reciprocity has to remain a mutual benefit for both parties in terms of respect. It also has multiple layers on how it is interpreted. Don't give your mind, body, and soul away to someone that takes advantage of the privilege of your presence. It'll never sit right with your spirit when someone you are interested in wrongs you and you allow yourself to repeat the same pattern. When the mask is off, take a peek into their nature and ask yourself if you are being tolerated or celebrated?

Reflection Questions:

Have you ever reflected on your tolerance level of others?

_____

_____

What did you learn about yourself and the other person?

_____

_____

On a scale from one to ten, how willing are you to repeat this pattern? Be honest.

_____

_____

Does it hurt to reflect on this? If so, it's OK to give yourself time to heal.

II

GIVING BIRTH TO THE WOMAN I WANT TO BE

> For everyone born of God overcomes the world. This is the victory that has overcome the world, even our faith." – 1 John 5:4

I never knew the power of valuing myself fully and unconditionally until I was forced to rid myself of toxic relationships and habits. I've learned that as women, we don't give ourselves enough credit when it's rightfully due. Not only are we hard on each other, but we are hard on ourselves. The moment we see our flaws as intricate details to a marvelous masterpiece we will begin to understand our being. God does not give us what we can't handle; He helps us handle what we are given.

Throughout the good and bad relationships I've encountered, there is one thing that remains continuous — how I treat myself. Not being so hard on myself was, and still is, tough. It's crazy how we can be mad at a person that disturbed our energy, but double that for ourselves. Thoughts of what we could have done differently, or if it was our fault in the slightest context can cause our minds to spiral. The irony in spiritual disruption is the sheer fact that those experiences play so vividly in our dreams and day-to-day processes. This is also the aftereffect of a soul tie that stretched further than its due date. No matter what you've gone through, the healing starts from within. Devote time and space for yourself and don't allow the energy of someone else to make way to overshadow your own. You are worth fighting for. You are a creation that was made to thrive and shine at maximum potential. Remember, don't harm your spirit by being your toughest critic.

Forgive yourself fully for anything you are frustrated about regarding your discernment of others. The reality is it's not coming back, but the beauty of it all is that you rose from that moment. Let it go. Lessons are necessary parts of life when we don't know any better because they teach us just how strong we are.

There is always a bigger picture, although I don't believe in struggle love, I do know sometimes experiencing adversity in any area helps build character.

Blessings come when you humble yourself and stop allowing the world to determine your morals. Just think, you're not who you used to be; you came out of that relationship whole. You are fearfully and wonderfully made and worthy of a mate that will love and honor you fully. Stop searching for what you already possess, in other people. Have faith in your journey and celebrate the little victories because they also have significance.

Loving yourself above all is the anchor for every other bond you form on the Earth. The way you treat yourself is the catalyst for how others will handle you. I realized early on that giving birth to the woman I still aim to be, keeps me grounded and alert from distractions. Let go of the fear of missing out, also known as 'FOMO', and step into your worth and wear it proudly. The very thing you let go of is probably what is blocking your biggest blessings. Ask yourself, is it worth it to lose yourself trying to hold on to temporary people or lose people and walk away with dignity?

12

MASTERPIECE I AM.

Thank you.
For not handling me with care as you once promised so many times over.
My heart,
once innocent, free, and without a doubt captivating.
Now isolated, seasoned, and like so much of the world, doubtful.
A Masterpiece should never be broken.
But in reality,
some of the world's biggest wonders are scarred, broken, and forgotten.
The definition of a masterpiece,
is a work of outstanding artistry, skill, and workmanship.
But the irony in your work,

is heavy brushstrokes that leave room for false promises.
Ha!
You thought that by dropping me I would glide off of the face of the Earth.
But I'm here to tell you that even pharaohs shine in a room full of darkness.
Although once stolen,
Mona Lisa smiles.
She remains captivating and unbothered.
You see my heart was never the sum of your lousy skills,
but the priceless prize you thought you could buy.
Redefined, Redeemed, and without a doubt, captivating.
My heart remains.

13

REBIRTH

"I can do ALL things through Christ who strengthens me." – Philippians 4:13

The time for change is now. There is so much hope for the future. With hard work, determination, faith, and resilience anything is possible. You have a resilient heart and deserve the best. It is up to you to realize that. Don't allow yourself to stay stuck in the same place as last year or yesterday. God has you covered and does everything for a reason. Walk in your purpose. The sadness you've felt inside will be no more. Stop focusing on people who don't put time and energy into you as you do for them. You are worth so much more. There is no space in your life for lies, worries, attitudes, fear of the unknown, and being taken for granted. The best things come to those who wait and the pleasures of life are paid in full to those who work for them. Bowing out of inconvenient situations should now be a specialty. So smile beautifully, from deep within, knowing that great things are in store. Keep God first, stay strong in your faith, and protect your heart of gold and your energy at all costs.

www.ingramcontent.com/pod-product-compliance
Lightning Source LLC
Chambersburg PA
CBHW071414290426
44108CB00014B/1825